THE BEST OF
MATT
2007

MATTHEW PRITCHETT

studied at St Martin's School of Art in London and first saw himself published in the *New Statesman* during one of its rare lapses from high seriousness. He has been the *Daily Telegraph*'s front-page pocket cartoonist since 1988. In 1995, 1996, 1999 and 2005 he was the winner of the Cartoon Arts Trust Award and in 1991, 2004 and 2006 he was 'What the Papers Say' Cartoonist of the Year. In 1996, 1998 and 2000 he was *UK Press Gazette* Cartoonist of the Year and in 2002 he received an MBE.

'Don't you just love the
wonderful stillness?'

The Daily Telegraph

THE BEST OF

MATT

2007

An Orion paperback

First published in Great Britain in 2007 by
Orion Books
A division of the Orion Publishing Group Ltd
Orion House
5 Upper St Martin's Lane
London WC2H 9EA
An Hachette Livre UK company

10 9 8 7 6 5 4 3 2 1

A CIP catalogue record for this book
is available from the British Library

ISBN 978 0 7528 8171 3

Printed and bound in Great Britain by Butler & Tanner Ltd,
Frome and London

The Orion Publishing Group's policy is to use papers that
are natural, renewable and recyclable products and
made from wood grown in sustainable forests. The logging
and manufacturing processes are expected to conform to
the environmental regulations of the country of origin.

www.orionbooks.co.uk

'How did sports day go?'

THE BEST OF
MATT
2007

'This media storm is a distraction from whatever it is we do here'

'Well, the sun's come up'

Prescott in trouble...

MPs sign letters calling for Blair to go

'Once a Prime Minister has set up residence it's almost impossible to get rid of him'

Brown criticised

'I have a new West Lothian
Question: how the
hell do I vote?'

'I'm just going to England
for a cigarette'

Poll confusion

'GET ORF MY LAND… and
can I count on your vote?'

'We think he may
have died laughing'

'I'm on eBay –
do you want a peerage?'

'Psst, are you guarding or
arresting today?'

Blair's tennis partner
questioned

*'I expect Lord Levy
could do with a hug'*

'I thought the cash for honours questioning should be handled more discreetly'

'I just need a peerage for my husband and I'll have finished my Christmas shopping'

'People forget that for dogs Tony Blair has been Prime Minister for 70 years'

'Do you want to cling on for coffee or leave while you're still popular?'

'Today we're going to build a lasting legacy for Tony Blair'

'It's stopped spinning and now it's going on a lecture tour of the US'

'Can you believe it? Tony Blair is STILL on his Farewell Tour'

'Can you wait six weeks? We're between leaders at the moment'

'He was the people's spinner'

'Don't worry, soon everything will be Gordon Brown's fault'

'So much for Gordon Brown's
new era – this back door
<u>still</u> sticks'

'When Gordon Brown
referred to a Cabinet of
all the talents…'

'If you let me arrest you,
then you can arrest me'

'We weren't expecting you
home this weekend; we've put
a prisoner in your room'

'Parole? I've been waiting months to get this cell and I'm not giving it up now'

'It's disgraceful, Home Secretaries seem to be able to come and go as they please'

'Half the department
has gone missing'

Department split in two

'It's an armed robbery.
Are you in the mood to go?'

'There's a cat stuck up a tree.
You can't object on
moral grounds'

Police priorities questioned

'We're very busy, so don't sneak off to the pub, George'

'My name's Miss Swann and I'll be teaching you physics'

Veil Row

'Well, the Britishness classes
seem to be working'

'A liquid bomb – and make it a double'

'Does the red traffic light mean this is high in salt, or that a terrorist attack is highly likely during breakfast?'

'Does he look
radicalised to you?'

'It's the latest advice for air passengers'

'Someone's been bringing dead birds into the house and it seems unfair to only check the cat'

'For security reasons we've lost your luggage'

'I got the idea from drug smugglers – I've swallowed our hand luggage'

Strikes on and off...

'Do we have to pay extra?
My husband has a lot of
emotional baggage'

'They need a lot
more check-ins'

'Ladies and gentlemen, we're being escorted back to Gatwick while we investigate reports of a crucifix on board'

'It's 50p for the deckchair
and £3.5 trillion for the
global warming'

'It's going to be hot and
sunny – I hope you're all
ashamed of yourselves'

'All those flowers must feel pretty stupid now'

'I left my TV on standby'

'The tree you planted to offset
our carbon emissions has just
been blown on to your car'

'I had to eat my Easter eggs
before global warming
melted them'

'We're being blown towards the
congestion charging zone'

London hurricane

Climate Change

'I walked back from the butcher. I'm shattered, but the chicken's cooked'

'If they introduce a methane tax we're done for'

'We're testing the effects of the £25 congestion charge'

Motoring

Parking tax

And finally...

'It's all those obese children going in the water'

'You should learn English and your son should gain four stone'

Obesity concerns

And finally...

'They're bred for their stupidity and aggressive nature and then put in a confined space to fight.'

'Going even further down than you thought was possible.'

And finally...

'My bank has charged me £35 for thinking unkind thoughts about it'

'It didn't go well. After bank charges and penalties, we owe them £247'

And finally...

And finally...

'Home Information Pack chaos: Lose will to live'

'Almost finished'

'Mrs Abramovich gets the players at weekends'

'Why police make always such bad decisions? For me is crazy mistake'

'I hope the logo will be finished by 2012.'

'I was wrong. The London Olympics is already bringing me enormous pleasure.'

'Paris is celebrating London
getting the 2012 Olympics'

'Dad, I'm giving up athletics,
I want to be a builder'

'Oi, take my dinner money, or else'

'I didn't get a place at my first choice school, but I've been offered IVF treatment'

'I shall now attempt to fail a GCSE'

CAPTAIN ☆ FANTASTIC

'Sometimes I wonder if the Department for Education really exists, or if everything is just random and pointless'

FAITH SCHOOL

Captured Sailors

'I'm mowing the lawn now and going to the pub later.' A shabby deal or a victory for quiet diplomacy? You decide'

DES BROWNE WALKS
THE PLANK

'Can I sell my story to the Bayeux tapestry?'

'Is it true that you have a different literary agent in every port?'

Captured Sailors

Royals

William and Kate

Harry and Iraq

'Her Majesty doesn't trust
mobile phones'

Mobile phone tapping

'Helen Mirren was fine as
the Queen, but I thought I
should have been played
by Meryl Streep'

'I only get drunk to make
myself look middle class'

'Sherry is SO dangerous.
Would you like an ecstasy
tab instead, vicar?'

'I don't have any child seats; this is only until you're 12!'

'We've got you surrounded. Do NOT come out until you've put on suncream!'

'Give it to me straight, doc, how long will my car have to spend in the hospital car park?'

'You can tell the "female" sperm; they stop and ask for directions'

Scientists create female sperm

'I like being unemployed – people think I'm a junior doctor.'

'Open wide.'

'Run over by a bin lorry –
what are the chances of
that happening?'

'I don't need a lift to the
polling station, but you could
take this sack of rubbish'

'This tall dark stranger –
will he be emptying
my dustbin?'

'It will be two weeks before I
can see you again, but I do see
some people privately.'

'You can talk on your
mobile phone now'

'It was a Porsche before I
put the faulty petrol in it'

'I was very careful at the office party to make sure I offended people of ALL faiths'

And finally...

And finally...

'They're not called insurgents,
minister, they're
called generals'

'I switched on the satellite navigation and moments later I was hit by a Chinese missile'

Chinese missile test

And finally...

'Moving the eggs from one aisle to another doesn't make them free range'

'It's a new breed of working dog – a Post Office pointer'

'George, you're upsetting
the budgie'

Bird Flu

'Faster! The lights
are dimming'

'......*till death or £48million us do part*'

Record divorce

'It's meant to be a Busy Lizzie...I seem to have grown a human heart'

Science breakthrough

And finally...

'Er...hi, Mum, I've sort of crossed the Atlantic, can you come and pick me up?'

Teenager crosses Atlantic

'We don't believe a heterosexual couple can provide a suitable home for a dog like this'

'You watch two episodes of The West Wing and suddenly you're an expert'

And finally...

'I owe your mother
an apology'

Postal charge changes

'Who am I? Am I the Bishop of Southwark?'

Tired and emotional bishop

'My husband opened our gas bill and exploded'

And finally...

And finally...

'*Something has to be done about these size-zero whippets*'

'*You know you're not allowed on premium rate phone lines!*'

'Are you carrying any
hair gel or baby milk?'

Russian assassination

'Will we be told if one of those
feral beast journalists moves
into the neighbourhood?'

And finally...

'A STORK BROUGHT ME?
I thought I came in
Madonna's private jet'

'And you should see the
replacement bus service'

'I happen to know that Desert Orchid faked his own death'

'We could parade pensioners on TV and force them to say we were treating them well'

And finally...

'It's pretty good,
but you're no Adolf Hitler'

Hitler painting sold